TOLKIEN'S REQUIEM

Concerning Beren and Lúthien

John M. Carswell

True Myths Press
P.O. Box 681163
Franklin, TN 37068
www.truemyths.org

TABLE OF CONTENTS

To my wife Greta for all of her support and to the incredible J.R.R. Tolkien for giving humanity his marvelous subcreations.

PREFACE

The following text is based on a paper I delivered in early 2014 at the University of North Alabama. The theme of the conference was "love and poison". When I first heard about the solicitation for papers for the conference, I immediately thought of the story of Beren and Lúthien. I had just completed my first read-through of *The Silmarillion* in the summer of 2013 (third time's a charm!), and I think I had doubled back to Beren and Lúthien at least once or twice, being entirely captivated by it.

Though Tolkien will forever be known chiefly for the classics *The Hobbit* and *The Lord of the Rings*, Beren and Lúthien is a marvel in its own right, and is a distant ancestor to both novels. Though it contains no trace of hobbits, it is a delight and

I will even say a *deserved* classic.[1] I might even suggest, as I have before, that if you have tried and failed to complete *The Silmarillion*, you should start with "Of Beren and Lúthien" first. It stands by itself, and, as I hope to show, it is a doorway into Middle-earth's First Age.

On that note, my intent here is to provide a reading of the story of Beren and Lúthien, and hopefully to open the door to the incredible depth and layered meaning contained therein. A caution however: this is only a proposed reading, and is most certainly not the only one possible. Tolkien chided those who tried to read his stories topically or allegorically. Frequent attempts were made to associate his works with the politics of his time, and Tolkien always denied that he wrote them with anything in mind other than the telling of a great story. As he put it, "To ask if the

---

1 I, for one, think that it would make an incredibly entertaining film.

Orcs 'are' Communists is to me as sensible as asking if Communists are Orcs" (*Letters* 262). In the works of Tolkien, an orc is an orc, and a ring is a ring. Assertions and observations contained herein are my own, unless specifically stated, and I dare not attempt to force this as the only possible reading.

Simultaneously, however, Tolkien was always willing to defend the applicability of his works. While he may not have been seeking to create orcs as a representation of anything else, it is entirely possible (Tolkien would say) that orcs are quite like Communists (and vice versa). Simultaneously, however, Tolkien might have admitted that a similar correlation existed between orcs and laissez-faire capitalists. There need not be a one-to-one rigid correspondence of symbolism for there to be a relatable understanding. As any statistician will tell you, correlation does not equal causation.

Thus, my intent here, in an attempt to be true to Tolkien's view, is to steer clear of saying that this is what Tolkien himself intended, unless, of course, there is a direct admission that he did in fact do so. Instead, my intent is to let you in on what my mind perceives when I read "Of Beren and Lúthien". I strive to be led closely by the text and the context of the work in doing so. I come to Tolkien's works as a total devotee, as one captivated by the marvel of his handiwork, something like the psalmist to the Torah and the oral tradition of Israel. I am here, dear reader, to help you see the glory of what I see in Tolkien's works.

In doing so, I hope to accomplish the following:

1) Introduce readers to the vast world of *The Silmarillion* in a way that is a bit more accessible than simply diving right in via "Ainulindalë".

2) Provide a worthwhile and illuminating exploration of the Tolkienian concepts of Escape, Recovery, Consolation, and Eucatastrophe in *The Silmarillion*.

3) Help the beginner to gain a sense of the overarching unity of the vast scope of *The Silmarillion*.

4) To convince my readers to read "Of Beren and Lúthien", either again or for the first time.

I would like to end this introduction with a few quick notes on the concepts of Escape, Recovery, Consolation, and Eucatastrophe.

Escape: Tolkien identifies "escape" as a crucial function of fantasy. In this, he opposes it to the idea of "escapism". Whereas escapism might seek to retreat and escape from the problems of this world, almost deny that they even exist, Tolkien likens the "escape" of fantasy to the prisoner seeking to escape the confines of his cell (*Tree and Leaf* 60). In other words, it is natural for humans to desire escape, and fantasy allows us to live out this desire.

Recovery: Tolkien believes that fantasy allows readers to *recover* a sense of a greater reality. He is not arguing necessarily for a materialist realism, but instead for a recovery of seeing things "as we are (or were) meant to see them" (58). For example, whereas the realist sees death as a negative end, in Tolkien's cosmogony death is a mystery and perhaps even a good (especially for Men).

Consolation: Tolkien identifies one of the chief ends of fantasy as "the consolation of the happy-ending" (68). Fantasy allows the reader to hope for ultimate happiness even amidst trials and hardships. In a world full of disappointment, death, and destruction, fantasy allows us to hope that these things might not have the final word.

Eucatastrophe: A word coined by Tolkien, eucatastrophe is the idea of the happy-turn, the lifting of the heart just as things seem at their darkest. In Tolkien's view, the twin eucatastrophes of human history are the Incarnation and the Resurrection of Jesus Christ (72). He pits it against "dyscatastrophe", what we are accustomed to thinking of as catastrophe, a disaster ending only in unhappiness.

These concepts play a highly important role in the story of Beren and Lúthien. Please keep them in mind throughout this book.

Finally, I'd like to make a brief note on the book's title. "Requiem" is probably a familiar word for most, one associated in my mind with music and sadness, but it actually has a rather definite meaning, which is significant for Tolkien. In the

Roman Catholic Church, of which Tolkien was a member, a Requiem Mass is said for the repose of the soul of one who has died. More generally speaking, a "requiem" can be some artistic form (musical or literary) intended as a tribute to another.

I had initially thought of calling this work "Tolkien's Epitaph", but that seemed just a bit too gloomy. Though the final title is a reference to Tolkien's epitaph (and of course his wife's as well), I believe Tolkien intended those brief epitaphs as requiems, as final words of a hope that reaches beyond *the confines of this world*. Thus, in unpacking the story behind those epitaphs, I hope to contribute to the singing of Tolkien's requiem in my own humble way.

A BRIEF INTRODUCTION TO CERTAIN NAMES

Throughout *The Silmarillion* one finds an incredible web of characters, a phenomenon that can leave the new reader (or even the veteran) with a spinning head. Here's a brief list of the most relevant figures and a short intro to each of them:

Beren: a mortal Man and warrior.

Lúthien: the immortal daughter of Thingol and Melian, she is a unique being in that she is the progeny of an Elf and a Maia.

Melkor (Morgoth): the most powerful of the Ainur who entered Arda (Middle-earth) in order to dominate and spoil it.

Ilúvatar: the Creator God figure of Tolkien's cosmogony.

Arda: the entire world that contains both Beleriand and Valinor.

Beleriand: the northwest lands of Middle-earth. These lands lie to the east of the Blue Mountains, which can be seen on the maps in *The Lord of the Rings*. They no longer exist after the First Age.

Sauron: a Maiar who was corrupted by Melkor before the First Age. He is essentially Melkor's right-hand man.

Telperion and Laurelin: The Two Trees of Valinor.

Fëanor: Elf of the Noldor, the most skilled maker among them, he is the creator of the Silmarils.

Valinor: The Blessed Realm, the home of the Valar in the West and the site of Telperion and Laurelin.

Huan: Great hound of Valinor given by the Valar to a son of Fëanor.

Carcharoth: A werewolf corrupted by Morgoth.

Thingol: Elvish king and father of Lúthien.

Melian: Maia queen, spouse to Thingol, mother to Lúthien.

Celegorm and Curufin: Sons of Fëanor who swear his oath and are thus committed to possessing the Silmarils.

Finrod Felagund: Elvish king who owes his life to Barahir, son of Beren, after the Battle of Sudden Flame.

A NOTE ON TEXT & STYLE

You'll notice that I begin each paragraph with its own number. Personally, I just enjoy the way this breaks things up. I hope you find it helpful, or at least don't mind it all that much.

'Then tell us some other tale of the old days,' begged Sam ' . . . the dark seems to press round so close.'

'I will tell you the tale of Tinúviel,' said Strider, 'in brief – for it is a long tale of which the end is not known . . . though it is sad, as are all tales of Middle-earth . . . yet it may lift up your hearts.'

The Fellowship of the Ring p. 187

Chapter 1

THE SEED OF MIDDLE-EARTH

"The kernel of the mythology, the matter of Lúthien Tinúviel and Beren, arose from a small woodland glade . . . in 1918." (*Letters* 221)

On the shared gravestone of J.R.R. Tolkien and his beloved wife Edith are written two names - "Beren" and "Lúthien". These are no mere pet names, but instead the names of two of Tolkien's *Silmarillion* characters, a pair of "star-crossed" lovers who forever changed the fate of Middle-earth by their heroic deeds, and are even recounted in poetic reference in Tolkien's masterwork *The Lord of the Rings*. Still, as can be

1

inferred from their placement upon the gravestone, they are very personal names as well. Upon Edith's death in 1971, Tolkien wrote:

> [In 1909] I met the Lúthien Tinúviel of my own personal 'romance' with her long dark hair, fair face and starry eyes, and beautiful voice . . . Now she has gone before Beren, leaving him indeed one-handed, but he has no power to move the inexorable Mandos, and there is no *Dor Gyrth i chuinar*, the Land of the Dead that Live, in this Fallen Kingdom of Arda, where the servants of Morgoth are worshipped.... (417)

Despondent though the quote is in its spousal anguish, it remains obscure for those unfamiliar with Tolkien's life's work, *The Silmarillion*. Tolkien's reference is, in fact, to the "seed story" of his sub-created "secondary world",[2] the epic

---

2 The concept of a "secondary world" is key to Tolkien's literary outlook. Tolkien aimed to create a fictional work

poem *The Lay of Leithian*,[3] first made known to the general public as a chapter in *The Silmarillion* entitled "Of Beren and Lúthien."

-2-

"Of Beren and Lúthien" is the tale of a mortal warrior and immortal princess who transcend the evil wrought by scheming foes and together fulfill a quest to recover a Silmaril, a great and precious jewel, the bride price of Lúthien's hand. It reveals Tolkien's own view of romantic love, of its pinnacle, and of its pitfalls and trade-offs as well. This text will examine the story from the perspective of a poison/love duality, and furthermore will expound upon the role of eucatastrophe in *The Silmarillion*. I will

---

that had an "inner consistency of reality," that could enchant the reader into feeling as though it were real.

3 *The Lay of Leithian* can be found in volume 3 of *The Lays of Beleriand*.

demonstrate that the love of Beren and Lúthien is the eucatastrophic force that puts right the great wrongs done by previous generations, though at great cost to the heroic pair themselves.

-3-

In 1939, Tolkien delivered a lecture at the University of St. Andrews in Scotland. In this essay, Tolkien, who had recently become famous as a writer of something like fairy tales with the publication and overnight success of *The Hobbit*, sketched out a literary theory of fantasy narrative and claimed that, when done rightly, it is "not a lower but a higher form of Art, indeed the most nearly pure form, and so (when achieved) the most potent" (*Tree and Leaf* 48). At the same time, Tolkien chided more allegorical or symbolical modes of fantasy for leaving little to the interpretation and imagination of the reader, and instead promoted a method he termed "subcreation" that focuses on creating a reality worthy of "secondary belief". The end result of such a work would likely result in something Tolkien identified and coined "Eucatastrophe", which he also called the "true form of fairy-tale, and its highest function" (68). Tolkien defined eucatastrophe as "the consolation of fairy-stories, the joy of the happy ending: or more correctly of the good catastrophe, the sudden joyous 'turn'" (68-69). He went on to further specify that eucatastrophe is not escapist in that "it does not deny the existence of dyscatastrophe, of sorrow and failure" but that these are necessary to its power as "a fleeting glimpse of Joy, Joy beyond the walls of the world, poignant as grief" (69). Thus, eucatastrophe is the happy turn catalyzed by some initial dyscatastrophe, the redemption after the fall, though mingled still with its own attendant sorrows and injuries. The concept of eucatastrophe – the "happy turn" – is key to Tolkien's fiction, as anyone who has read *The Hobbit* or *The Lord of the Rings* can probably recognize. A hint: for Tolkien, eucatastrophe often involves eagles.[4]

-4-

"Of Beren and Lúthien" takes place in a fallen world, a world that has lost the great light of the Two Trees of Valinor, Telperion the Silver and Laurelin the Gold. The very title *The Silmarillion* comes from the story of the great elf-lord Fëanor, the "fiery spirit", who crafts three unbreakable jewels and fills them with the glorious light of these Two Trees. His creations are the marvels of all, though they receive such attention that Fëanor quickly becomes suspicious of admirers and seeks to hide them away from all except his closest kin in an effort to protect them. When the dark lord Melkor (known in the story of Beren

---

4 Why eagles? I think it has to do with the Eagles being creatures of the air, and of the Valar of the air, Manwë, being the High King of Middle-earth under Eru Ilúvatar. They miraculously intervene because they represent the mysterious will of Ilúvatar himself.

and Lúthien as Morgoth) and the hideous spider-demon Ungoliant poison Telperion and Laurelin, the Silmarils are all that remain of their light, and the only hope of restoring them. Nevertheless, Fëanor refuses to surrender the Silmarils to the great powers (the Valar, quasi-angelic beings) of Valinor, and when Melkor murders his father and steals the three Silmarils, Fëanor and his sons swear an unbreakable oath that none shall ever possess the Silmarils except for them. Fëanor and his kin (the Noldor) depart Valinor in anger and pride, murdering their weaker kinsmen and stealing their ships. In sum, centuries of war and sorrow are set off by these three great dyscatastrophes: *the poisoning of the Two Trees*, *the theft of the Silmarils*, and *the Kinslaying*. These are not the first falls in the long history of Middle-earth, though they are perhaps the most significant for the purposes of the tale of Beren and Lúthien. With these incidents, the action of The Silmarillion shifts from the Blessed Realm of Valinor (across the sea in the east) to Beleriand, in the northwest of Middle-earth.

-5-

The proper account of Beren and Lúthien takes place many years later, long after Fëanor has perished at the hands of Morgoth's forces. Beren emerges as the last survivor of a band of mortal warriors, and, encountering the immortal Lúthien, seeks her hand. The great elf-king Thingol, Lúthien's father, requires that Beren obtain a Silmaril from Morgoth's crown as Lúthien's bride price, a seemingly impossible task, yet, through the aid of Lúthien and the mighty wolf-beast Huan, they succeed against all odds at finally obtaining a single Silmaril, though at the cost of their lives. Such is often the fate of the heroes in Tolkien's world: though a victory is achieved, the hero is unable to enjoy its spoils.

-6-

Beren and Lúthien's story is ultimately a great eucatastrophic light amidst multiple, building dyscatastrophes. Their love serves to counteract the poisonous effects of the numerous dyscatastrophes that precede it and surround it, events often driven by a poisoned love, that is, a love that is misdirected or selfish. Before examining the story of Beren and Lúthien proper, it will be helpful to gain a brief understanding of the dyscatastrophes surrounding the Silmarils themselves, as this will help to illustrate how the stage is set for the eucatastrophe of Beren and Lúthien. The next chapter will present a brief history of the events that lead up to the time of Beren and Lúthien, and set the stage for the events of their story.

Chapter 2

FËANOR, MELKOR, AND THE TRAGEDY OF THE TWO TREES

"Thus began the Days of the Bliss of Valinor; and thus began also the Count of Time." (Silmarillion 39)

From the beginning, the world (Arda or Middle-earth) is endlessly lit by the Lamps of the Valar. One is situated in the extreme north; the other is situated in the extreme south. Together they create "a changeless day" (35). However, Melkor, in a great assault, throws the lamps down and their lights are broken and the lands of Arda are horribly marred. Yavanna – Valier of growing things – and Nienna – Valier of tears – together create The Two Trees of Valinor—Telperion and Laurelin. They become the new sources of light for the western world. What follows is an age of joy, not

10

only for the quasi-angelic beings of Valinor but also for the Elder Children of Ilúvatar, the Elves, who are drawn to the light from across The Great Sea. When Manwë, Valinor's king, summons the Elves, it is so they might, with his people, enjoy the light of the Two Trees forever.

-8-

The Two Trees of Valinor are contrasting and complementary and they seem to be typologically oriented to the two races of The Children of Ilúvatar. Telperion is the elder. He is silver, and one of his flowers eventually becomes the Moon. Laurelin is gold, and one of her fruits eventually becomes the Sun. It is the emergence of the Sun that awakens Men, whereas the Elves awoke under starlight, and thus the Moon "cherishes their memory" (99).

-9-

Melkor, never content with the destruction he has previously wrought, sets out to destroy the

Two Trees of Valinor with the aid of Ungoliant.
Ultimately, his design is not so much the
destruction of the Two Trees as it is the
possession of the Silmarils and the ruining of the
Elves, whom he hates. Tolkien relates the murder
of the Two Trees thusly:

...[T]here came the mingling of the lights,
when both Trees were shining, and the silent
city of Valmar was filled with a radiance of
silver and gold. And in that very hour Melkor
and Ungoliant came hastening over the fields
of Valinor, as the shadow of a black cloud
upon the wind fleets over the sunlit earth;
and they came before the green mound of
Ezellohar. Then the Unlight of Ungoliant rose
up even to the roots of the Trees, and Melkor
sprang upon the mound; and with his black
spear he smote each Tree to its core,
wounded them deep, and their sap poured
forth as it were their blood, and was spilled
upon the ground. But Ungoliant sucked it up,
and going then from Tree to Tree she set her

black beak to their wounds, till they were
drained; and the poison of Death that was in
her went into their tissues and withered
them, root, branch, and leaf; and they died.
(*The Silmarillion* 75-76)

While Ungoliant's poison deals final death to the
trees, it is Melkor's hatred of the Valar, hatred
motivated by a prideful self-love, which occasions
their death. Yet even so, there is a certain lust
that factors into Melkor's action as well. His
designs reach beyond the destruction of the Two
Trees into a desire for possession. Previous to this
episode, Tolkien had attributed to Melkor an
intense "lust" for the Silmarils:

Then Melkor lusted for the Silmarils, and the
very memory of their radiance was a gnawing
fire in his heart. From that time forth,
inflamed by this desire, he sought ever more
eagerly how he should destroy Fëanor and
end the friendship of the Valar and the Elves;
but he dissembled his purposes with cunning,

and nothing of his malice could yet be seen in
the semblance that he wore. (67-68)

Melkor wants to possess the jewels in such a way
that prevents others from possessing them.[5] This
is Melkor's chief flaw from before the
foundations of Arda: for him, love means
possession and domination, the need to hoard
and to guard a treasure as one's own. In fact, in
"Ainulindalë", we learn that Melkor seeks to
increase his own power and glory when he is
already the most powerful and glorious of created
beings. It seems that his own greatness leaves
him jealous of the potential of others, with a
need to see others always as a threat to his own
glory. Thus, he must possess the Silmarils lest
someone else do the same instead of him. In
truth, however, Melkor is not the only one to
have such a possessive reaction to the Silmarils.
Of Fëanor, Tolkien says that he "began to love

---

5 This harkens back to the description of him from
Valaquenta or Ainulindalë.

the Silmarils with a greedy love, and grudged the sight of them to all save to his father and his seven sons; he seldom remembered now that the light within them was not his own" (69). Thus Fëanor is slowly corrupted by an illicit desire of possession. The light of the Silmarils, taken as it is from the Two Trees, is a light belonging to no individual or group of individuals but common to all. It is quite literally a light that fills the world. When Fëanor creates the Silmarils, he captures and contains something previously free to all. Though Melkor is the first to explicitly desire the Silmarils for his own, Fëanor and others soon follow suit. Thus, Fëanor's love for the light of the Two Trees poisons the light by containing it, by making it scarce, when all along it is something that should not be contained. His desire and action to possess the blessed light sets into the hearts of the story's free agents the will to possess it singularly and selfishly.[6]

---

6 It is interesting that the final solution to the problem of the light is to take one of the fruits of the two trees and set it

-10-

Ungoliant is an enigma and no easy read. Whereas from the beginning of the mythology Melkor is a vainglorious figure obsessed with domination, Ungoliant, on the other hand, is a mysterious figure of unknown origin, once corrupted to darkness by the seductions of Melkor, but having since repudiated his service for her independence.[7] Yet despite her independence from Melkor, she hates the peoples of Valinor all the same. As Tolkien puts it, she is a figure "desiring to be mistress of her own lust, taking all things to herself to feed her emptiness" (73). Still, Melkor knows her deepest need, a desire to be filled by all things. He finds

in the sky, where it may indeed be common to all and free from the desire for selfish possession. (99)

7 The Silmarillion never gets 100% clear on this matter, but it sounds as though she was one of the Maiar corrupted by Melkor, as noted in the Valaquenta.

her in the dark caves to the south of Valinor, desperately hungry for the light of the Two Trees but hating it all the same, fearful of it and of the Valar who tend it (73). When he promises her fullness of the Light, she sets forth to do his bidding. Melkor wounds the trees, "and their sap poured forth as it were their blood, and was spilled upon the ground," presenting Ungoliant with her feast (76). She sucks up every last drop of the Trees' light-blood, bloating to a prodigious size, yet famished evermore. Ungoliant's love is turned inward, seeking always fullness, but unable to find it. Acting alone, she is a poison to herself only; under the influence of another, she is a poison to many.

-11-

Ungoliant is a nightmare, a hellish vision of self-absorption worthy of Dante. For all that she devours, for all that she poisons, for all that she ruins, she is absorbed by her own hunger and need, at once desiring light but hating it all the same. Tolkien gives us little to go off of with

17

regard to Ungoliant. We do not really know how she took this form, from what estate she fell, only that she was likely corrupted at some time past by Melkor. The same is true of her fate; all we know is that she forsakes Melkor again, and that "some have said that she ended . . . when in her uttermost famine she devoured herself at last" (81). In Dante's terms, if Melkor belongs among the wrathful, then Ungoliant has been fixed into the permanent state of the gluttonous, who love sensual pleasure yet hate it all the same.

-12-

The destruction of the trees causes the Valar to turn their minds to the Silmarils in the hope that their light might be used to heal and restore the trees before it is too late. Yet Fëanor laments; should he surrender the light of the Silmarils, the Silmarils themselves would cease to be: "It may be that I can unlock my jewels, but never again shall I make their like; and if I must break them, I shall break my heart, and I shall be slain; first of all the Eldar in Aman" (78). In the same instant, the poisonous whisperings of Melkor "returned to him, saying that the Silmarils were not safe, if the Valar would possess them" and Fëanor refuses outright to hand over the Silmarils (79). Yet before even more controversy can come of the Silmarils, Melkor and Ungoliant steal them from the vault of Formenos, murdering Fëanor's father, the Noldor King Finwë, in the process. Melkor (renamed Morgoth, "the Black Foe of the World", by Fëanor and referred to by this name henceforth) flees with the Silmarils and escapes across The Great Sea to his dungeon-palace, Angband. Melkor has accomplished all that he designed: he has pitted the Elves against the Valar and obtained the Silmarils for his own possession. His victory is complete, and leaves Valinor, the once Blessed Realm, in confusion, darkness, and filth.

-13-

Having accomplished Melkor's aims, it does not take long for the criminal partners to turn on one another. Ungoliant desires to devour the

Silmarils, yet Melkor wants to possess them. Though Ungoliant briefly overpowers Melkor, his minions, the Balrogs, hear his anguished cries and emerge from Angband's depths to deliver their master. At this, Ungoliant flees, not only from the story but also from history itself. The last we learn of her is that she is the mother of those giant spiders that will come to inhabit both Mirkwood and the pass of Cirith Ungol (Shelob herself). Melkor and Ungoliant are something like the antithesis of the Two Trees. Whereas the Two Trees provide light and waters to nourish the hallowed things of Valinor, Melkor and Ungoliant bring darkness and filth with a choking heaviness. It is not simply that they shut out the lights; they bring a substance all their own, with the power to strangle the will. When one considers the impressionistic description of Shelob's lair – that it was a place where "night always had been, and always would be, and night was all" – one can know better what the darkness of Melkor and Ungoliant really was (*The Two Towers* 702).

-14-

Fëanor's response to the death of his father and the loss of the Silmarils leads to the third dyscatastrophe. Setting himself finally against the Valar, he summons the Noldor, Elves of his own kin, to continue the pursuit of Morgoth across the Great Sea. He calls them to a vow that will haunt them for the rest of their days:

> They swore an oath which none shall break, and none should take, by the name even of Ilúvatar, calling the Everlasting Dark upon them if they kept it not; and Manwë they named in witness, and Varda, and the hallowed mountain of Taniquetil, vowing to pursue with vengeance and hatred to the ends of the World Vala, Demon, Elf, or Man as yet unborn, or any creature, great or small, good or evil, that time should bring forth unto the end of days, whoso should hold or take or keep a Silmaril from their possession. (83)

21

Though Fëanor indeed hates Melkor as much as (perhaps more than) any other figure, he is also quite like him. Fëanor often seems overly concerned with his own status and protective of his glory. At one point previous, he threatens his younger half-brother, Fingolfin, in the sight of many, accusing him of seeking to usurp his rightful status as heir to the throne of their father, Finwë. One can see this same spirit of jealousy and possession in the words of the oath. Though Fëanor is the greatest of all the Children of Ilúvatar in talent, he is ever wary of his status, much like Melkor, and therefore must guard it jealously, and, if need be, bring destruction to those who would stand in the way of his aims.

-15-

Great ill comes of the oath, for it leads to a stand-off between the army of Fëanor and their Elvish brethren, the Teleri, who refuse to grant them use of their ships in crossing the Great Sea to pursue Morgoth. A battle is joined, in which

22

many of each side perish, an event ever after known as the Kinslaying. Yet Fëanor and his brethren finally obtain many ships, and undertake their voyage of pursuit across the Great Sea. What follows is a long story of great sorrow, of the lamentable outcomes of Fëanor's Oath.

-16-

One begins to detect in the examples of Melkor, Fëanor, and even Ungoliant the attitudes of the spirit that are seen in later figures. The keenest example of this is Gollum. Gollum must possess Sauron's Ring. In one way, his need to possess it reflects Melkor's own jealous attitude. For another to possess the Ring is unacceptable and means that he will not be able to possess it. In another way, he is like Ungoliant, not really possessing so much as being possessed by it to his utter end and destruction. No matter what the object of lust and jealousy is – Sacred Jewels, Ring of Power, Arkenstone – the need to possess, to have the object of love, results in a disorder

23

that leads to catastrophe and tragedy.

-17-

We will also come to see that Melkor is like the dragons of later years, seeking to possess to no truly profitable end. To possess the Silmarils is to deprive others of their life-giving light, much like, for Smaug, to possess the Lonely Mountain is to deprive the dwarves of their kingdom and their treasure. Possession for them is about both personal glory and depriving others. Indeed, Melkor retreats into Angband only to emerge once again, content like Smaug to simply hoard his treasure to himself. And like all those who possess Sauron's Ring, Melkor comes to find that his prized possessions are a great weariness to him, though he would never part from them. Indeed, evil is a wearying and heavy thing, though not easily broken with.

-18-

Though Melkor, unlike Ungoliant, had a motive

for obtaining the Silmarils that went beyond mere possession, now that he has them and his revenge upon the Valar, he becomes increasingly Ungoliant-like, becoming inwardly focused, seeking only to cast further darkness. His will is slowly diminishing, and his life-force passing away, though, as the greatest of Ilúvatar's creations, he has plenty to spare.

Chapter 3

FURTHER DYSCATASTROPHES

"Thus it was that as Mandos foretold to them in Araman the Blessed Realm was shut against the Noldor . . ." (*Silmarillion* 102)

The peoples of Fëanor (the Noldor) come to inhabit the lands of Beleriand in the northwest of Middle-earth, often doing battle with the forces of Morgoth. They frequently find themselves in tense relations with the Moriquendi, those Elves who had never made the voyage to Valinor and are so named because they had never seen the Light of the Two Trees.[8] At some later point, the younger, mortal Children of Ilúvatar, Men, cross the mountains

---

8 Calaquendi = Elves of the light; Moriquendi = Elves of the darkness. These terms refer to the light of Valinor.

into Beleriand for the first time, and come into contact with the Elves. Some of these men join forces with the Elves against Melkor and are rewarded with kingdoms of their own in the Elvish lands. Among these Houses is the House of Bëor, and descended from Bëor is Barahir, the figure who opens the chapter "Of Beren and Lúthien."

-20-

Men are known as the Younger Children of Ilúvatar. Whereas Elves are granted natural immortality, Men are given mortality as a gift. In the letter preceding the main text of *The Silmarillion*, Tolkien claims that Mortality is one of the chief concerns of the entire saga, especially as it "affects art and the creative . . . desire" (xiii). While we as mortal Men might indeed look longingly upon the immortality of the Elves, Tolkien makes it clear that natural death is a gift given to Men by Ilúvatar. It is by death that they escape the sorrows and weariness of life that otherwise cause the Elves to suffer greatly down through the ages as the world around them withers away and their life force is dispersed.

-21-

In the same letter, Tolkien says that one of the chief ways in which the creative desire can become corrupted is that it may "become possessive, cling to the things made" (xiii). It seems that this desire for possession is closely related with the nature of mortality for Tolkien. If my horizons do not go beyond this life, my goal is to possess as much as I can in the here and now, or simply to protect my possession of what I already have. For Tolkien, possessiveness seems to be a form of misguided self-love.

-22-

Barahir and his band of twelve are survivors of the Battle of Sudden Flame, a catastrophic conflict that unleashes Morgoth's forces upon Beleriand. Barahir's men become guerilla warriors after the battle, and are effective enough to warrant Morgoth's attention. Morgoth charges his chief lieutenant, Sauron (yes, THAT Sauron), with the task of ending Barahir's campaign. Sauron succeeds in doing so by manipulating one of Barahir's men—Gorlim the Unhappy:

> His wife was named Eilinel, and their love was great, ere evil befell. But Gorlim returning from the war upon the marches found his house plundered and forsaken, and his wife gone; whether slain or taken he knew not. Then he fled to Barahir, and of his companions he was the most fierce and desperate; but doubt gnawed his heart, thinking that perhaps Eilinel was not dead. At times he would depart alone and secretly, and visit his house that still stood amid the fields and woods he had once possessed; and this became known to the servants of Morgoth. (162)

Gorlim becomes an easy target for the ruthless methods of Sauron, who tempts Gorlim into treachery with visions of his wife and promises of reunion. Gorlim finally relents, betraying the whereabouts of Barahir and his men in the vain hope of seeing Eilinel again. Sauron shows that he has learned well the power of suggestion from his master. As Fëanor's heart was ultimately poisoned against the Valar by Melkor's insistent falsehoods, so Gorlim's resolve is broken down by the empty promises of Sauron. Sauron exploits the sickened love of Gorlim, gaining the knowledge he needs and then putting Gorlim "cruelly to death" that he might join his beloved (163). Gorlim is the story's first victim of poisonous love. The hopes of his heart are used against him, treacherously twisted into a trap.

-23-

Gorlim is, by the book, a traitor. Though we know little about him beyond this episode, it is clear that he fails his comrades. Tolkien does not necessarily leave this hard fact as a judgment in and of itself though. After all, Frodo was a failure in the strictest sense, an "apostate" as Tolkien put it in a 1956 letter to Michael Straight of *The New Republic*. "He gave in, ratted," Tolkien says of the Ring-bearer (*Letters* 326). At the same time, however, Tolkien urges caution in pronouncing a moral judgment upon his protagonist. After all, the Ring's power essentially crushed Frodo's will and drove his mind to the point of madness. Thus, we see then that pity and mercy are weighty factors in Tolkien's moral assessment. So too we might apply the same standards to Gorlim, who has witnessed much in the way of hardship and sorrow, and whose will is finally broken by the tortures of the enemy. After all, his last known action is in Beren's dream, where he at least seeks to warn Beren of the impending danger to the other warriors. Though Gorlim's last known effort is too little and too late, we can see that Gorlim is a victim of lies and deception and not simply, in Tolkien's eyes, a hopeless traitor.

-24-

Having thus gained knowledge of Barahir's

31

whereabouts, Morgoth's forces ambush and executes them, save one—Barahir's son, Beren. When he learns of his father's death, Beren swears "an oath of vengeance" (163), and for the next four years lives as a solitary outlaw in the wilderness, becoming so feared for his exploits that whole armies of Orcs would flee rather than seek him out. It is during this period that he stumbles upon Lúthien, the elvish princess, "as she danced upon the unfading grass in the glades beside Esgalduin" (165).[9] Yet their love would not be had so easily. Coming before the throne of Lúthien's father, the Elven king Thingol, Beren receives his bride price: a Silmaril from the Iron Crown of Morgoth. Queen Melian then utters prophetic words:

'O King, you have devised cunning counsel. But if my eyes have not lost their sight, it is ill

---

9 This scene was apparently the root inspiration for the whole tale. Tolkien recalled it late in life, after the death of Edith, as a vision borne of personal experience. (*Letters* 420)

for you, whether Beren fail in his errand, or achieve it. For you have doomed either your daughter, or yourself. And now is Doriath drawn within the fate of a mightier realm.' (168)

Though Thingol insists that he has the matter entirely in hand, one cannot escape the significance of the bride price he has set. He has offered to exchange his own daughter, the "being of Light", "the fairest of all the Children of Ilúvatar that was or ever shall be" for one of Fëanor's accursed jewels, the last bit of the scarce light of the Two Trees (56). Thingol's devices have become too complicated. Though he may congratulate himself on setting an unattainable price, in doing so he has become like Sauron, who wickedly exploited Gorlim's love for Eilinel as a murderous trap. Furthermore, there is in the bride price the hint of Fëanor's Oath and of the blood spilled in his rage, as well as the lust of Melkor. Thingol, who had once grasped for love himself when he wooed Melian (herself "a Maia, of the race of the Valar"), fails to recognize in Beren the same spirit that once possessed his own heart, and for which he forsook the Light of Valinor (55). Furthermore, his designs demonstrate that he has turned from the pure love of self-giving to the poisoned love of possession.

-25-

Beren's task is literally drawn into the Oath of Fëanor when he is detained in Nargothrond, the elvish kingdom ruled by Finrod Felagund. In the Battle of Sudden Flame, Barahir had rescued Finrod from death, an act that left the immortal Finrod mortally indebted to Barahir's line. Nargothrond is also the home of two of the sons of Fëanor, Celegorm and Curufin, who revolt at the notion of any obtaining a Silmaril but those bound by Fëanor's oath. When Finrod seeks aid for Beren's mission from the Elves of his kingdom, Celegorm arises and recalls the oath:

'Be he friend or foe, whether demon of

Morgoth, or Elf, or child of Men, or any other
living thing in Arda, neither law, nor love, nor
league of hell, nor might of the Valar, nor any
power of wizardry, shall defend him from the
pursuing hate of Fëanor's sons, if he take or
find a Silmaril and keep it. For the Silmarils
we alone claim, until the world ends.' (169)

Thingol's trap has been sprung more quickly than
he had imagined, and the Sons of Fëanor are set
against Beren and his task before Morgoth or
Sauron even know of it. Celegorm's vow recalls
the fierce jealousy which motivated Fëanor's
Oath, the mixed venom of bitterness, distrust,
selfishness, and pride that led to the Kinslaying
upon the shores of Alqualondë.

-26-

Celegorm and Curufin are recurring characters in
the story of Beren and Lúthien. Celegorm's
jealousy goes beyond the Silmarils themselves,
and he seeks to possess Lúthien. Through
pretenses of concern and assistance, he entraps

Lúthien (who has fled her father's kingdom to save the imprisoned Beren) and uses her bondage to press Thingol into helping him obtain Finrod's throne. Though Lúthien obtains her freedom by the aid of the mighty wolfhound Huan, the schemes of Celegorm and Curufin are hardly at their end. They later waylay Beren and Lúthien after Lúthien's rescue of Beren from the dungeon of Sauron, and with great hatred nearly succeed in murdering Beren. When Lúthien forbids Beren from slaying Curufin in vengeance, Curufin, in a vengeful act of desperation, lashes out at Lúthien:

> But Curufin, being filled with shame and malice, took the bow of Celegorm and shot back as they went; and the arrow was aimed at Lúthien. Huan leaping caught it in his mouth; but Curufin shot again, and Beren sprang before Lúthien, and the dart smote him in the breast. (177)

Desperate and jealous, Fëanor's sons, like Melkor

and Ungoliant, lash out against the light of Lúthien the fair. They do so out of wrath, out of a foiled desire for the power that comes with the princess' hand, and also in hatred of her light, that which they desire but blinds them. If they cannot have her, and the power that comes with her, then none shall.

-27-

Furthermore, Celegorm's vow draws back into the tale the poisoned love of the Silmarils, and drives Celegorm and Curufin to conspire against their elvish kin[10] with the aim of assailing Morgoth with all the forces of Beleriand. Another kinslaying is perhaps averted by the love of Beren and Lúthien, especially when Thingol learns of Celegorm and Curufin's designs. Though Thingol is enraged and seeks war with their kingdom, he learns they are no longer welcome in

---

10 Thingol is of the same race as the Teleri, the victims of the Kinslaying, and is the brother of Olwë their king.

Nargothrond, and so relents.

-28-

It seems as if each character has taken some oath by which he is bound. The Sons of Fëanor own their father's rash oath; Beren vows to avenge his father's death; Finrod is bound to fulfill his oath to Barahir. The oaths come to symbolize a sort of prideful and self-centered myopia. They create dilemmas that force immoral actions rather than the seeking of the common good. They lead to the shedding of blood when it might not have been necessary. One begins to sense that any oath uttered in *The Silmarillion* is a foreshadowing of disaster and perhaps even the fruit of a flawed character. Though oaths are uttered for the purpose of committing oneself to some important mission or goal, they seem rather to bind a character to eventual disaster and poor choices. One hears the words of St. James echoing in the results of these oaths: "Do not swear, either by heaven or by earth or with any oath, but let your yes be yes and your no be no, that you may not fall under condemnation." Oaths are an add-on, a prideful sort of guarantee, a way of saying, "I will do better than simply 'Yes.'" Still, oaths cannot simply be seen as evil things in and of themselves. A wisely considered oath can bind people together in a great cause, and can be a way of reminding a person what they are ultimately called to do. Yet the characters of *The Silmarillion* seem quite adept at making rash oaths, oaths based not on fulfilling some greater good but based instead on protecting one's self-image. In this way, they are relatable to the historical case of Beorhtnoth, whom Tolkien considered in a 1953 academic work "The Homecoming of Beorhtnoth Beorhthelm's Son." Beorhtnoth, leader of the Anglo-Saxon forces, foolishly gave his enemies free use of a key bridge in order to establish a level playing field. He almost seemed to view battle as sport rather than a matter of life-and-death. Tolkien chastises the hubris that led to such a decision, claiming instead "It is the heroism of obedience and love, not of pride or wilfulness, that is the most heroic and the most moving" (*Tree and Leaf* 148). An oath is only good if it is based in love of another, and not in love of self.

-29-

Amidst all of the catastrophes catalyzed by the creation of the Silmarils and their theft by Morgoth, it is ultimately the virtuous love of Beren and Lúthien that leads to redemption and the symbolic re-kindling of the light of the Two Trees. Though more (and greater) dyscatastrophes occur in the story, these further dyscatastrophes bear consideration within the context of Beren's mission.

Chapter 4
THE EUCATASTROPHE OF BEREN AND LÚTHIEN

"Among the tales of sorrow and of ruin that come down to us from the darkness of those days there are yet some in which amid weeping there is joy and under the shadow of death light that endures." (Silmarillion 162)

Beren's desire for Lúthien comes first. He happens upon her in the wild borderlands of Thingol's kingdom. At first, she is a healing balm to his weary soul: "Then all memory of his pain departed from him, and he fell into an enchantment; for Lúthien was the most beautiful of all the Children of Ilúvatar" (165). Soon, however, her elusiveness becomes a sort of poison to him, a paralyzing force:

41

But she vanished from his sight; and he became dumb, as one that is bound under a spell, and he strayed long in the woods, wild and wary as a beast, seeking for her . . . And he saw her afar as leaves in the winds of autumn, and in winter as a star upon a hill, but a chain was upon his limbs. (165)

Beren experiences "escape" at the sight of Lúthien. He has for some time lived the miserable life of an outlaw, always on the run, knowing hunger, cold, exposure, and the feeling of being hunted. It has been an ugly and hard life, the life of a prisoner. Though he remains free in body, he is imprisoned in a wilderness of constant fear. Thus, Lúthien's "enchanting" effect is the sight of beauty, of holy light. In *On Fairy-Stories*, Tolkien speaks to "enchantment" as one of the key effects of good fantasy. Lúthien is something like true freedom in and of herself, an embodiment of healing and love. It is as if Beren is reminded by Lúthien's presence of all of the good for which he once fought, perhaps even of a good that goes beyond the confines of this world. In Lúthien, he finds a mission greater than mere survival. Eventually, Lúthien falls for Beren, and their fates are joined:

> As she looked upon him, doom fell upon her, and she loved him; yet she slipped from his arms and vanished from his sight even as the day was breaking. Then Beren lay upon the ground in a swoon, as one slain at once by bliss and grief; and he fell into a sleep as it were into an abyss of shadow, and waking he was cold as stone, and his heart barren and forsaken. And wandering in mind he groped as one that is stricken with sudden blindness, and seeks with hands to grasp the vanished light. (165)

There are echoes of the first stage of courtly love here, of "deadly joy" and of "happy pain" as Andrea Hopkins terms it in *The Book of Courtly Love*. It is notable that Tolkien says that "doom" fell upon her when she first looked at him.

"Doom" is a term used quite frequently by Tolkien; it connotes fate and judgment, but not necessarily in a negative sense, as we are used to hearing it used in contemporary society. Instead, Tolkien seems to be saying that Beren's love and admiration and her reciprocation of it brought upon Lúthien something not necessarily proper to her—the fate of death: "Being immortal, she shared in his mortality, and being free received his chain; and her anguish was greater than any other of the Eldalië has known" (165-166). Yet she freely chooses this anguish because she chooses Beren and his mortality.

-31-

It is not surprising that Beren falls for Lúthien, as she is, after all, the most beautiful of The Children of Ilúvatar. Yet what does she see in Beren that draws her to him? He may be a great warrior, but he is a mortal and a stray. It would seem that Beren's effect on Lúthien comes from his calling to her: "Tinúviel." When she hears this name, meaning "nightingale", escape his lips, she

44

falls for him. What does she hear in this word and in his voice? Perhaps it is a secret name that she already knew. Perhaps she finds in him one pitiable yet full of unprecedented nobility. It could be any number of things, yet the text (as well as Aragorn's poetic account in *The Fellowship of the Ring*) leaves her "fall" mysterious. All we know is that at this word she sees him and his doom falls upon her. It would seem that fate has ensnared her. Much like Frodo, who willed not that the One Ring should come to him but was instead ensnared in its fate, so too Lúthien willed not her love of Beren but was ensnared in his fate for some greater purpose.

-32-

Beren's "chain" is significant. The immortality of Elves (the Firstborn Children of Ilúvatar) and the mortality of Men (the Younger Children of Ilúvatar) is one of the central tensions of Tolkien's mythology. Though it may seem counter-intuitive to mortals like us, natural death

45

is, in fact, viewed as a "gift" to Men within the tales of Middle-earth (*The Silmarillion* 42). As the Elves and the Valar live through countless ages, the burden of life becomes wearisome, even a sorrow, especially as the blessed light of Valinor fades. In a way, Lúthien's receiving of Beren's "chain" is the first eucatastrophic turn, a choice of pure love requiring humility, over and against the pride of the immortal races, and shows forth Lúthien as a redemptrix. Simultaneously, it is an act of wisdom, a sober recognition of the burden of immortality in a sorrowful world; ultimately, it is also an escape.

-33-

It seems strange to speak in one paragraph of Lúthien's "fate" and of her "choice" at the same time. We are accustomed to thinking of these two things as opposing qualities, as liquids that cannot mix. Yet to use the case of Frodo again, though he is ensnared in the fate of the One Ring, he must ultimately choose to carry through his mission to the end. So too with Lúthien, it as if she knows, upon hearing Beren's voice for the first time, that she has been called away from her pleasant life in the woodland paradise of Doriath into the woeful life of Beren. Perhaps this is why she flees him after their initial embrace: she sees in him a fate of sorrow and of death. She must find the resolve to choose this path, and so ultimately "she laid her hand in his" (166). Though fated, she must freely choose her doom, not as one of many options, but as a loving sacrifice.

-34-

Nevertheless, they enjoy a brief time of joy, their love hidden from all others. However, this happiness is soon betrayed to Thingol by the jealousies of Daeron[11] the minstrel, who "also

---

[11] Daeron is an interesting figure that is not developed at great lengths. Elsewhere he is spoken of as the mightiest of singers of the First Age (*Silmarillion* 254). Nevertheless, his love of Lúthien acts as a poison as well, as he jealously betrays her infatuation to her father.

loved Lúthien" (166). Daeron's betrayal is a
catalyst for the racial[12] displeasure of Thingol,
who views Men as unworthy even of the service
of Elves, much less the hand of his daughter,
whom "he loved above all things" (166). Yet
Beren, by the mysterious aid of Melian, finds
these words for Thingol:

> 'My fate, O King, led me hither, through
> perils such as few even of the Elves would
> dare. And here I have found what I sought
> not indeed, but finding I would possess
> forever. For it is above all gold and silver[13],

---

12 Thingol could be accused of many "-isms" here, including
"classism", "immortalism" and "racism". We don't really have
a word in our own reality for Thingol's view of mere mortals
like Beren. It is stated, however, that Thingol does not even
employ mortal Men. Perhaps the "-ism" is ultimately a
hatred of death, a hatred of Men because they stink of the
possibility of death.

13 Notably, The Two Trees of Valinor are described as
"Laurelin the gold" and "Telperion the silver." Thus, Beren's
statement implies that he prizes Lúthien above all of the

and beyond all jewels. Neither rock, nor steel, nor the fires of Morgoth, nor all the powers of the Elf-kingdoms, shall keep from me the treasure that I desire . . .' (166)

Again, the question of possession is present. For Beren, Lúthien is a thing to be possessed; though he is the object of her reciprocated love, he is, at this point, one more dog in the fight, one more individual who views Lúthien as a thing to be possessed, much as Fëanor sought to possess the light of the Trees and Melkor sought to possess the jewels themselves. Beren, actually possessing Lúthien's love (in comparison to the jealous love of Daeron and others), unwittingly mimics the Oath of Fëanor, who actually possessed the right to the Silmarils but allowed his jealousy of the beloved jewels to poison the joy and the love of

---

things over which the Valar, the Elves, and Morgoth have battled.

them.[14] Thingol relents, and assigns Beren his quest:

> 'Bring to me in your hand a Silmaril from Morgoth's crown; and then, if she will, Lúthien may set her hand in yours. Then you shall have my jewel; and though the fate of Arda lie within the Silmarils, yet you shall hold me generous.' (167)

------

14 It is possible that I am being too hard on Beren here. After all, it should not seem unusual that an ancient warrior would seek to "possess" the heart of a fair princess. Though it strikes against modern sensibilities for a father and a suitor to be speaking of a woman in terms of "possession", it might seem even stranger for characters in an ancient story not to do so, an anachronism if you will. However, I find Lúthien, and in reality many of Tolkien's female characters, to be strikingly in line with certain modern feminist notions. They often come to the rescue of clumsy and foolish men; they are often paragons of wisdom; and they don't really like being hemmed into a tight corner. Furthermore, despite Beren's foolishness and Thingol's cunning, she nevertheless loves them both and seeks to do right by them. In sum, I think my analysis of Beren's motives stands.

The pride remains overwhelming. Thingol expects Beren to praise his generosity. Beren vows against "the fires of Morgoth" and "the powers of the Elf-kingdoms" in what should be a simple request for Lúthien's hand. There is no ability to find the common good. Every player is self-interested. Beren might be headed down the same road as Fëanor at this point.

-35-

Though Thingol's bride price is Beren's quest, Lúthien is wrapped into it from the outset (remember her "doom"), and when Beren is captured by Sauron and thrown into a dungeon, she senses his peril from afar, and escapes her own imprisonment (at the worried hands of Thingol) to assist him. In the first of the three great eucatastrophic scenes, Lúthien, with the aid of Huan the mighty wolfhound, assails the fortress of Sauron, first summoning Beren from his misery with "a song that no walls of stone could hinder" (174). Eventually, her song causes the isle upon which the fortress is set to tremble, summoning Sauron in the form of a werewolf, of whom Huan makes quick work. When Sauron flees, Lúthien, with Huan, stands triumphant:

> Then Lúthien stood upon the bridge, and declared her power: and the spell was loosed that bound stone to stone, and the gates were thrown down, and the walls opened, and the pits laid bare; and many thralls and captives came forth in wonder and dismay, shielding their eyes against the pale moonlight, for they had lain long in the darkness of Sauron. (175)

Lúthien's assault frees not just Beren, but numerous other prisoners. It is fascinating that so much of what she is able to accomplish comes by song, for it is in music after all that the Ainur (aka the Valar and the Maiar) were first created. When Lúthien sang in the woods of Doriath, it melted the "bonds of winter" causing flowers to spring beneath her feet. Lúthien's song is one of creative power, able to set prisoners free and to warm the winter. In a way, her song would be the most complete of all songs, for as both a Maia and a Child of Ilúvatar, she sings of things not envisioned by the Ainur.

-36-

It is also notable that Felagund, an unfortunate Elf that dies in Sauron's dungeon, had fallen prisoner after a duel of song, apparently at the recollection (in theme) of Fëanor's Kinslaying.[15] Sauron poisons the triumphant song of Felagund by bringing to mind the past misdeeds of the

---

15 In a sense, memory of the Kinslaying would be particularly troublesome for Finrod, because he is descended from all three lines of the Eldar: his mother, Eärwen, is daughter of Olwë, king of the Teleri; and his father, Finarfin, is Noldorian on his father's side and Vanyarian on his mother's side. Thus, memory of the violent sundering of the elvish brotherhood strikes at the very root of who he is. He embodies the unity of the three Calaquendi peoples.

Noldor.[16] Thus, just as music is a creative force in Tolkien's cosmogony, it is also a force capable of destruction, just as Morgoth used it in the Music of the Ainur to assert his own will and glory.

-37-

Though Beren and Lúthien enjoy a brief period of reunited love, Beren recalls his oath to Thingol, and sets out once again for Angband, the fortress of Morgoth. Preceding this second eucatastrophe, Lúthien insists upon accompanying Beren. Though Beren curses his oath to Thingol, Huan speaks prophetically (a special, limited grace he was given by the Valar): "'From the shadow of death you can no longer save Lúthien, for by her

---

16 Music is foundational to the cosmogony of Tolkien. The world first comes into being through the "Music of the Ainur." The Elves awaken singing on the shores of Lake Cuiviénen. It should come as little surprise then that much of the battling is done in song, whether it be to Felagund's tragic outcome or Lúthien's power over the chains of Sauron.

love she is now subject to it'" (179). It is becoming clearer how the love they share has become a poison to Lúthien's immortality, for she cannot stand to be parted from him, even as he plunges toward danger. His doom has truly become hers.

-38-

Their encounter with Morgoth again centers more upon the deeds of Lúthien than of Beren. As had occurred at the sight of the Silmarils, Morgoth "looking upon her beauty conceived in his thought an evil lust, and a design more dark than any that had yet come into his heart since he fled Valinor", though his lust becomes his undoing (180). He accepts Lúthien's offer to sing for his court, and by her song a deep slumber falls upon all present. She wakens only Beren, bidding him cut a Silmaril from the crown of Morgoth. When they escape with a Silmaril, they are confronted by the great hellhound Carcharoth, who attacks Beren, and bites off and

devours the hand that holds the Silmaril.
Carcharoth flees, and Eagles[17] rescue Beren and
Lúthien from the pursuit of Morgoth's forces.

-39-

Carcharoth has been bred against all nature to a
prodigious size, and by Morgoth "he became
filled with a devouring spirit, tormented, terrible,
and strong" (180). And just as Ungoliant sought
to devour the light of the Two Trees that she
hated, so Carcharoth, at swallowing the Silmaril,
is "filled with a flame of anguish" (181).
Carcharoth is the dyscatastrophic force
unleashed by Beren's quest. As a beast of
Morgoth, Carcharoth is a perversion. As the
original orcs were, in fact, Elves imprisoned and
tortured beyond all recognition, so Carcharoth is
a pup fed on living flesh and forced to grow too

---

17 Eagles are frequent players in eucatastrophic events. They
are creatures of Manwë, King of the Valar, the being closest
to Ilúvatar.

fast. Again, Morgoth is not capable of true subcreation, only of mockery and perversion.

-40-

The final eucatastrophe centers upon the hunt for Carcharoth, who has set a destructive path through the countries of Elves, an unholy beast filled as he is with the fire of holiness. After Carcharoth attacks Beren, Huan attacks Carcharoth and the two beasts battle to their deaths. Ultimately, the venom of Carcharoth's bite mortally wounds Huan, a poisoning he ultimately suffers after "the love of Lúthien had fallen upon him in the first hour of their meeting" and he had come to her aid, imprisoned in Nargothrond (173). And Beren too suffers death, but not until the Silmaril is retrieved from the belly of the dead Carcharoth. At its retrieval, "the hand of Beren that held the jewel was yet incorrupt" (186). No explanation for Beren's incorrupt hand is made, yet it harkens back to the instance at which he first came to possess the Silmaril: "As he closed it in his hand, the radiance welled through his living flesh, and his hand became as a shining lamp; but the jewel suffered his touch and hurt him not" (181).

-41-

What are we to make of the reaction of the Silmaril to Beren? The matter is not entirely clear, yet it seems as if it must be speaking to the purity of Beren's motive for possessing it. After all, when Morgoth had first stolen the Silmarils from the vault of Formenos, "they had begun to burn him" as they did the belly of Carcharoth (80). Where Morgoth's motive was to possess the jewels themselves (mingled of course with hatred of the Valar and of Fëanor), Beren's motive went beyond the Silmaril. In a sense, Beren passes a test by preferring Lúthien's love to the possession of a Silmaril. Though, as has been stated previously, Beren may not have the best of motives for his quest, his motives are ultimately purer than Thingol's, for instance, who is willing to use his daughter's hand as bait in exchange for one of the accursed jewels. Beren ultimately has his values in order: person over object.

-42-

The motive for possessing something is a theme that runs deep throughout Tolkien's works. When one considers the various figures that possess the One Ring, one can see this illustrated. Gollum murders his cousin in order to obtain the Ring for himself, and thus becomes a wretched shadow of his former self. Bilbo obtains the Ring without any sort of treachery, though he feels compelled to lie to justify his ownership of it. Frodo obtains the Ring only for a sacred mission, but even over time desires to possess the Ring selfishly and, as a result, fails in his quest. It is only Sam who ultimately seems to come away unscathed from the Ring, and only after possessing it for little time, and after being shored up by his self-sacrificial attendance to Frodo. Sam is the only Ring-bearer who desires nothing like possession of the Ring, and for this reason, he is the least burned by it. Notably, Tolkien mentions the motive of possession as one of the "falls" a subcreator may suffer in making something (xiii). We may surmise from these other instances that a subcreator may be subject to possessiveness of the creations of others as well.[18]

-43-

Even despite the Silmaril's favorable reaction to him, has Beren changed? Remember: when he first receives Thingol's bride price, his taking of an oath to "possess" Lúthien calls to mind Fëanor. Has Beren been humbled by his quest? After all, it is not by his mighty deeds that a Silmaril has been gained, but by the wisdom and heroic virtue of Lúthien and Huan. Left to his own devices, Beren would have soon met his end in the dungeon of Sauron. This reality is further symbolized by Beren's injury from Carcharoth. Though he briefly possesses the Silmaril,

---

18 *Covetousness* is probably a better word than possessiveness for desiring the creations of others.

Carcharoth rips it from his grasp once again, and it is only by the final aid of Huan that Beren's hand is recovered and his mission accomplished. Beren the mighty is brought low, and though he lives long enough to see his quest finally fulfilled, and the bride price of Lúthien paid, he nevertheless meets his end and suffers the loss of the love he had already been freely given. Beren, though triumphant in his quest, pays a heavy price for his pride and possessive desire.

Chapter 5

CONSOLATION

"Is everything sad going to come untrue?" (*Return of the King* 930)

As mentioned previously, Tolkien had spoken of eucatastrophe in *On Fairy-Stories* within the context of something he termed "consolation". He spoke of fantasy as having an altogether different final function than drama. Where drama is focused on tragedy, and in particular the tragedy of death, the fairy-story goes beyond death to "the Consolation of the Happy Ending," something that "all complete fairy-stories must have" (*Tree and Leaf* 68). He relates this in a beautiful way:

> It is the mark of a good fairy-story, of the higher or more complete kind, that however

wild its events, however fantastic or terrible the adventures, it can give to child or man that hears it, when the 'turn' comes, a catch of the breath, a beat and lifting of the heart, near to (or indeed accompanied by) tears, as keen as that given by any form of literary art, and having a peculiar quality. (69)

What then is the consolation of the lovers Beren and Lúthien? After all, though they have succeeded in fulfilling Beren's quest, he has passed away into darkness, and Lúthien, in sorrow, falls asleep. In the end, did all of this happen only for the purpose of tragedy, so that Thingol might obtain a Silmaril? While Morgoth and Sauron have suffered defeat, they are not finally defeated. Is there a happy ending to this story?

-45-

After his death, Beren's spirit tarried in what are called the Halls of Mandos, awaiting Lúthien's presence there. In itself, this is remarkable, for it was not the fate of mortal Men to enter into these halls at death, but to pass from this world with ambiguity, perhaps to return at the end of time, after the final cataclysm. Yet by some mysterious assistance from Lúthien, it was so. And when Lúthien came to Mandos, she pled for Beren's spirit, and Mandos was uniquely moved to pity by her song:

> [It was] the song most sorrowful that ever the world shall hear . . . For Lúthien wove two themes of words, of the sorrow of the Eldar and the grief of Men, of the Two Kindreds that were made by Ilúvatar to dwell in Arda, the Kingdom of Earth amid the innumerable stars. (187)

Once again, Lúthien's song serves as a salvific force, a means of release for the prisoner. Furthermore, in blending the stories of the two races, the song recalls that blending of the light of the Two Trees that brought joy to all of Valinor. It is significant then that the song "is sung still in Valinor beyond the hearing of the world," for it comes to symbolize the awakening of the sympathies of the Valar that will eventually bring about the final downfall of Morgoth.

-46-

Still, Mandos is bound by the word of Manwë. He cannot simply grant Lúthien her desires. Manwë receives mysterious guidance from Ilúvatar, and Lúthien is given a choice: dwell in Valimar until the world's end, forgetting all of her griefs, including Beren; or return to Middle-earth with Beren and become subject to natural death. She chooses Beren, and consequently mortality, "forsaking the Blessed Realm," yet despite the certain doom that this casts upon her it is in her that the Two Kindreds shall be joined in flesh, and the fate of Middle-earth will be forever changed. Lúthien's choice is the decisive turning point in the downward spiral initiated by Morgoth and exacerbated by Fëanor. Though it is not the end of sorrow and of bloodshed in Middle-earth, it is, as Gandalf would say, the turn of the tide.

-47-

Thus, Beren and Lúthien return to Beleriand, though hidden from most of their kindred, living a life together until their deaths. From their line springs a combined race, though their descendants must ultimately make the same choice as Lúthien—mortality or immortality. From their line will spring Elrond and Arwen. Also, by the mortal line of Elrond's brother Elros, Aragorn descends.

-48-

Their granddaughter Elwing plays an important role in the ultimate downfall of Morgoth, for she carries Thingol's Silmaril back to the Blessed Realm. Along with her husband, the mariner Eärendil, they convince the Valar and the Teleri to come to the aid of the peoples of Beleriand, and to assault Morgoth once again. In this assault, Morgoth is thrown down forever, imprisoned beyond the walls of the world, never able to personally wage war against it again.

-49-

As Aragorn descends from them as well, it is seen that their love plays a considerable part in the downfall of Sauron, though many years later. Aragorn, after all, plays a major role in the defeat of Sauron.

-50-

In what way does their love put right the dyscatastrophes of the Two Trees? Though Lúthien's light fades from the world when she chooses mortality, her choice yields the mingled light of the Two Kindreds of Ilúvatar, a light that will accomplish much toward the defeat of evil in the ages to come. Furthermore, in the union of Two Kindreds, there is a symbolic repairing of the wounds that sundered the Elves at the

Kinslaying,[19] as well as the eventual reparation of the friendship of the Valar and the Elves of Middle-earth. The deeds of Beren and Lúthien are deeds unto reunion and the putting away of darkness.

-51-

Still, Lúthien's mortality is a deep wound for the elves, and especially for her father, Thingol, and her mother, Melian. Though she is able to visit Thingol briefly and "heal his winter . . . with the touch of her hand," Melian "looked in her eyes . . . and knew that a parting beyond the end of the world had come between them, and no grief of loss has been heavier than the grief of Melian the Maiar in the hour" (188). The eucatastrophic joy of Beren and Lúthien is not a final happiness, for even Beren and Lúthien must both die and be

---

19 Not to mention consolation for the death of Finrod Felagund, elf of the three Quenya races, who was ultimately slain because of the memory of the Kinslaying.

parted from this life. In a 1956 letter to Michael Straight of *The New Republic*, Tolkien wrote these insightful lines:

> I think that 'victors' never can enjoy 'victory' – not in the terms that they envisaged; and in so far as they fought for something to be enjoyed by themselves (whether acquisition or mere preservation) the less satisfactory will 'victory' seem.[20]

In this brief quote the unique heroism of Lúthien specifically, even against Beren, becomes even clearer. All the time Beren fights to fulfill his vow, i.e. his right to possess Lúthien. She, on the other hand, condescends to his mortality in order to

---

20 Frodo faces a similar reality. Despite his heroic stature, he is not able to enjoy the spoils of his victory in the same way that Sam, Merry, and Pippin are. Upon their parting at the Grey Havens, he tells Sam, "It must often be so, Sam, when things are in danger: some one has to give them up, lose them, so that others may keep them." (*Return of the King* 1006)

rescue Beren from himself and his hasty vow. Hers is not the poisonous, self-absorbed desire of possession, but the self-giving love of other for the other's sake. Though she is ultimately a 'victor', her enjoyment of 'victory' is fleeting, and not something that she can envision on her own terms.[21] Though she will spend some time with Beren, she will, like him, eventually suffer death.

-52-

It is remarkable then to return to the inscription on the Tolkiens' gravestone. Tolkien's desire to name Edith "Lúthien" and himself "Beren" comes off as nothing less than a tribute to the woman

---

21 She is her mother's daughter. It is Melian who is quick to provide Beren with the words to speak to her husband. Though she of all the characters has the strongest prophetic sense, she nevertheless knows that Beren and her daughter are destined for greater things and for the aid of others, and intervenes to ensure Beren's mission, even though she knows that in this she will lose that which is most precious to her.

who saved him, returning from the horrors of war in 1917. Furthermore, we might even understand it as Tolkien's own twist upon the traditional "requiescat in pace" or "rest in peace". Tolkien is invoking the hope of a joyful reunion, a victory that he cannot envisage in this life. This would, of course, have been in full accord with Tolkien's Catholic beliefs, where every week the hope of "the resurrection of the dead and the life of the world to come" is confessed. After all, in *On Fairy-Stories*, Tolkien referred to the Resurrection of Jesus Christ as one of the two "Great Eucatastrophes" of human history (*Tree and Leaf* 73). While to Tolkien's mind there is no "land of the dead that live" in this fallen world, he seems instead to look forward to this new reality, and a joyful reunion there.

-53-

Though Tolkien eschewed attempts to "symbolize" or "allegorize" his stories, one cannot help but connect the dots and call the story of Beren and Lúthien Tolkien's most personal. In it, we are able to glimpse most clearly his own ultimate hopes and desires, and to find our hearts resonating with his as we attempt to see in our own poisoned ways of loving the possibility of redemption by a greater love outside ourselves. In a world that seems as dark, if not darker, than the world of Tolkien's reality, we find ourselves searching for our own Lúthiens, beings of light and of self-sacrificial love. When we suffer the death of a loved one, our hearts seem to reach beyond the imprisonment of the grave for the hope of blessed reunion. If the story of Beren and Lúthien and its significance in Tolkien's life are any indication, then we do so with him.

POSTSCRIPT

As I stated at the outset, my aim with this short exposition was to illuminate for the reader one of Tolkien's greatest stories and to provide a backdoor into *The Silmarillion*. My hope, then, is that you will proceed from here to a full reading of that great work, for my goal, at the end of the day, is to open up Tolkien's profound mind to you. To that end, I hope that you are satisfied with the job that I have done, and I invite you to visit my website TrueMyths.org, which is devoted to a similar unpacking of Tolkien's works and of the wisdom contained therein.

John M. Carswell
December 2014

WORKS CITED

Hopkins, Andrea. *The Book of Courtly Love*. San Francisco: Harper San Francisco, 1994. Print.

Tolkien, J.R.R. *The Fellowship of the Ring*. New York: Houghton Mifflin, 1994. Print.

Tolkien, J.R.R. *The Letters of JRR Tolkien*. Ed. Humphrey Carpenter. New York: Houghton Mifflin, 2000. Print.

Tolkien, J.R.R. *The Return of the King*. New York: Houghton Mifflin, 1994. Print.

Tolkien, J.R.R. *The Two Towers*. New York: Houghton Mifflin, 1994. Print.

Tolkien, J.R.R. *The Silmarillion*. Ed. Christopher Tolkien. New York: Houghton Mifflin, 2001. Print.

Tolkien, J.R.R. *Tree and Leaf*. London: Harper Collins, 2001. Print.

Made in the USA
Columbia, SC
11 January 2019